Favorite Pieces for CLASSICAL GUITAR

ISBN 978-1-4768-1289-2

WILLIS MUSIC

EXCLUSIVELY DISTRIBUTED BY

HAL•LEONARD®
CORPORATION
7777 W. BLUEMOUND RD. P.O. BOX 13819 MILWAUKEE, WI 53213

Visit Hal Leonard Online at
www.halleonard.com

CONTENTS

Canon in D

By Johann Pachelbel
Arranged by Keith Gehle

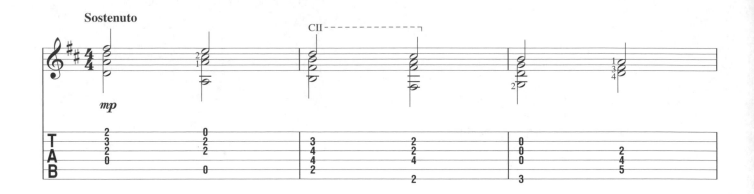

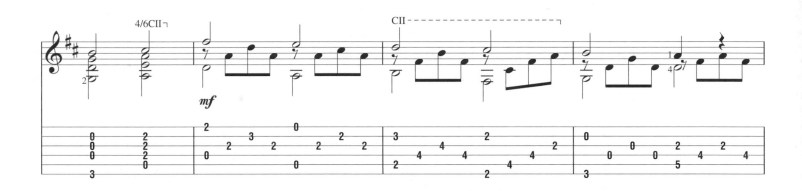

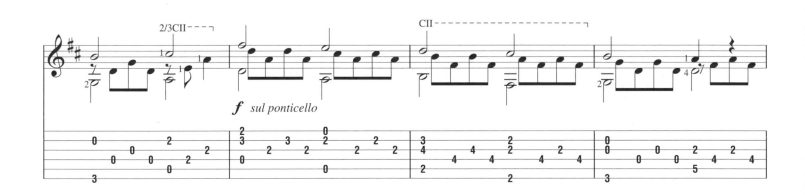

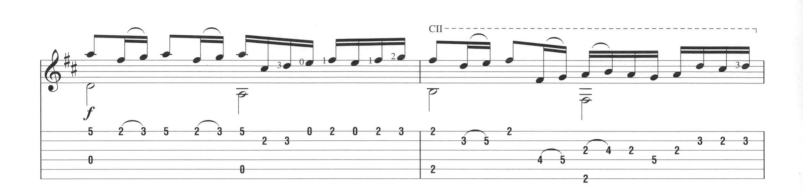

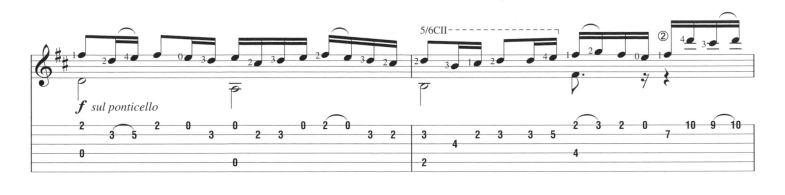

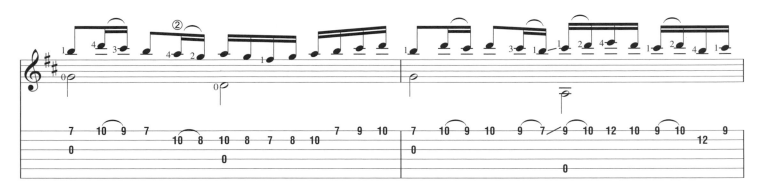

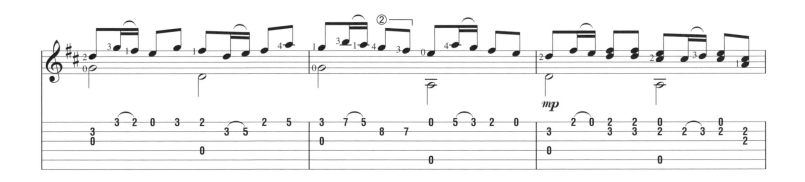

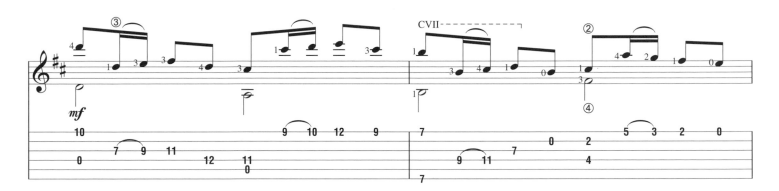

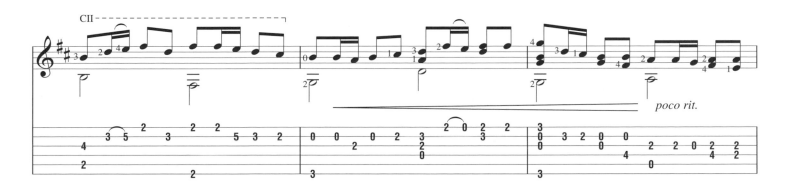

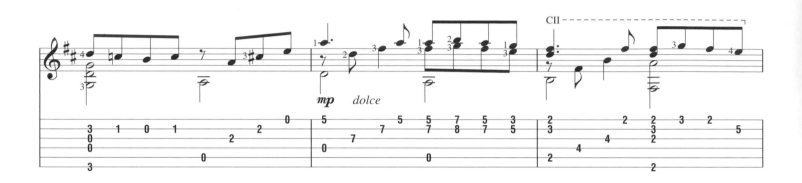

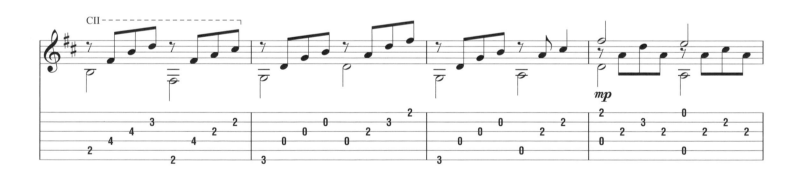

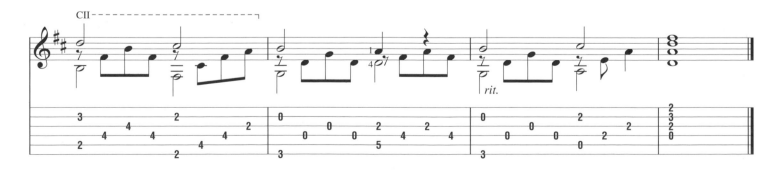

The Entertainer

By Scott Joplin

Transcribed for Guitar by Elias Barreiro

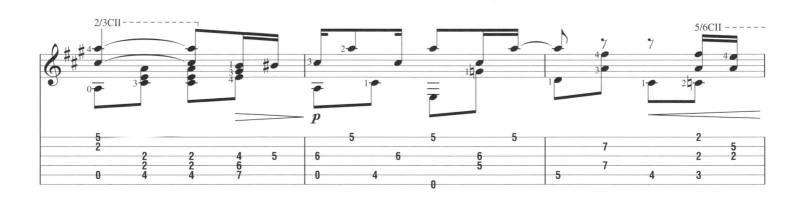

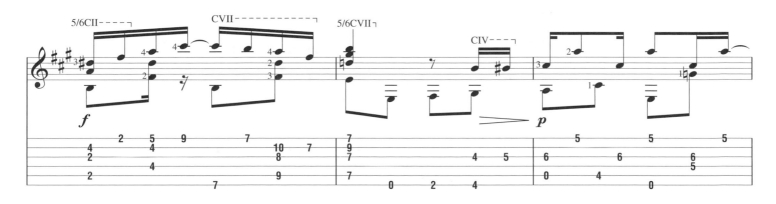

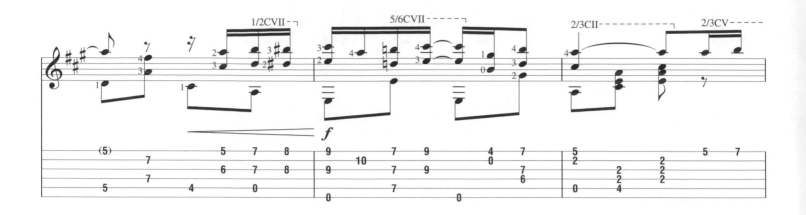

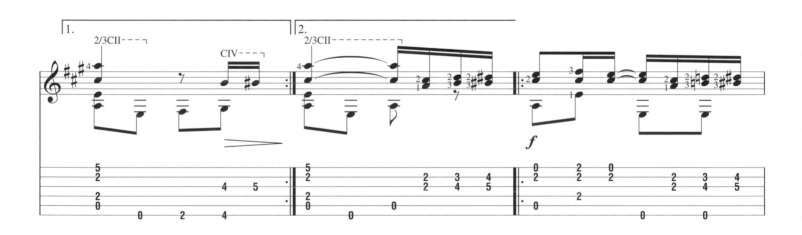

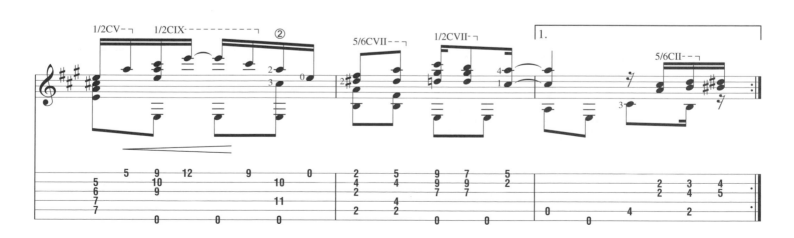

11

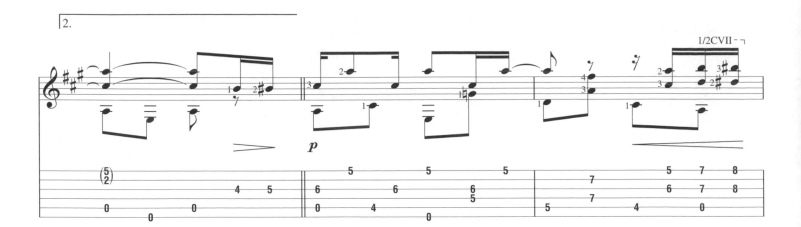

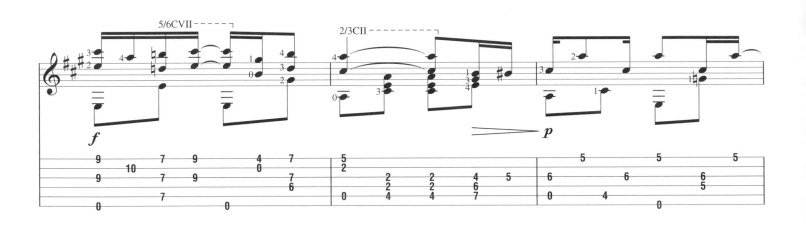

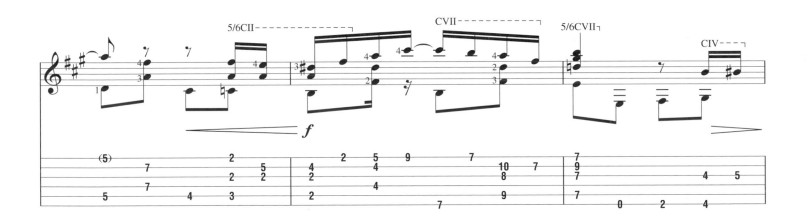

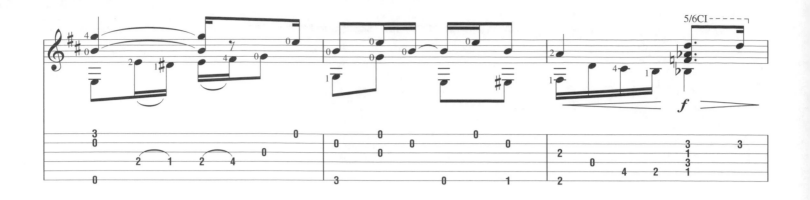

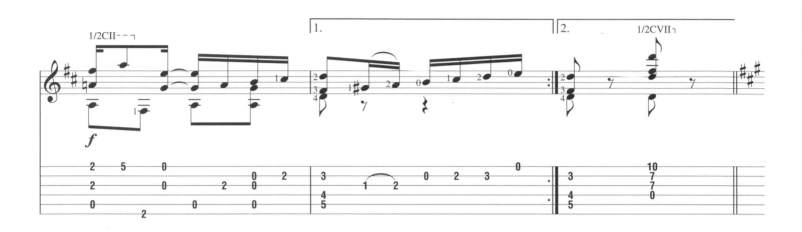

Clair de Lune

By Claude Achille Debussy

Arranged by Robert Henley Woody and Julius Bellson

Andante

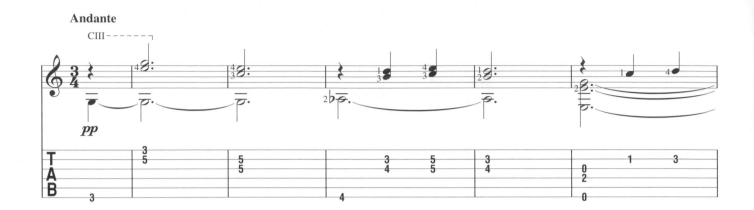

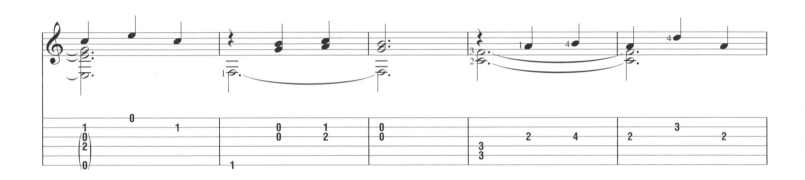

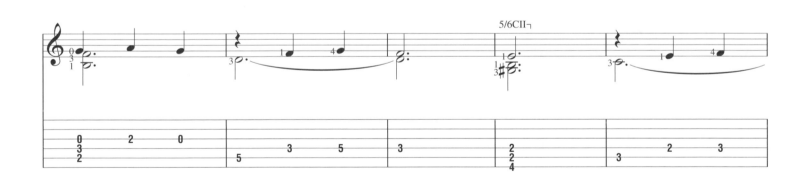

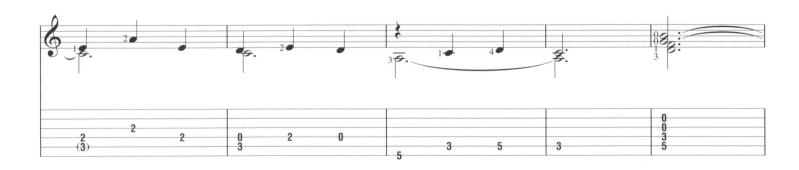

Für Elise
(For Eloise)

By Ludwig van Beethoven
Arranged by Robert Henley Woody and Julius Bellson

Greensleeves

Traditional English Melody
Arranged by Giovanni De Chiaro

Jesu, Joy of Man's Desiring

Chorale from CANTATA 147
By Johann Sebastian Bach
Adapted for Guitar by David Dolata

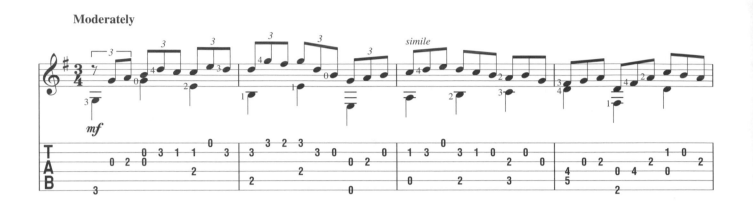

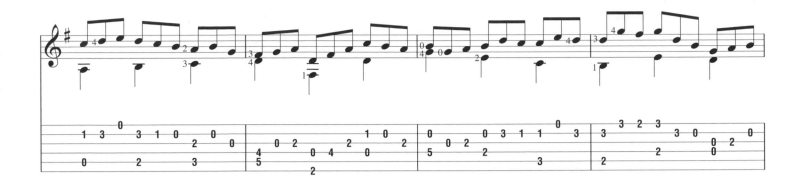

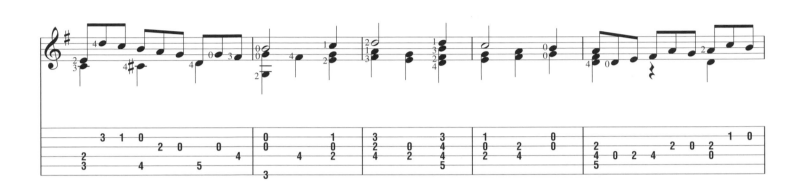

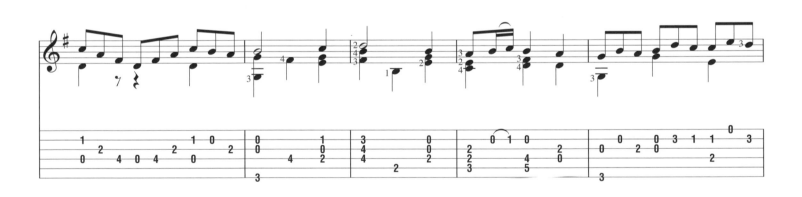

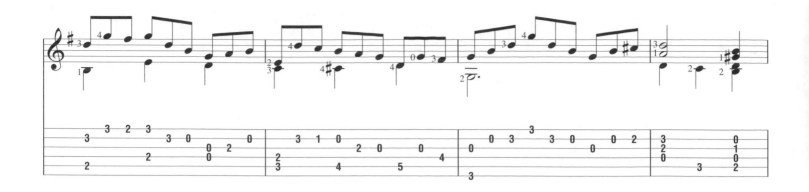

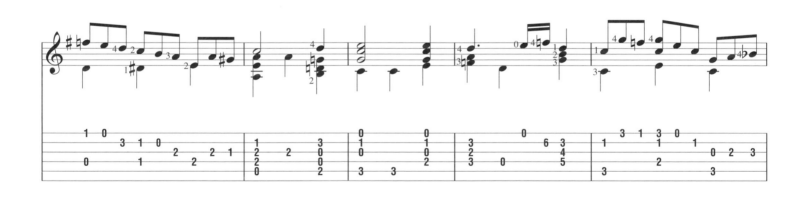

Maple Leaf Rag

By Scott Joplin

Transcribed for Guitar by Giovanni De Chiaro

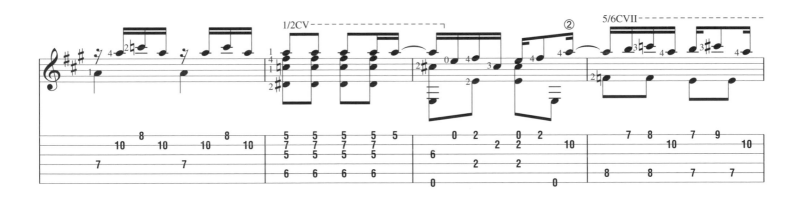

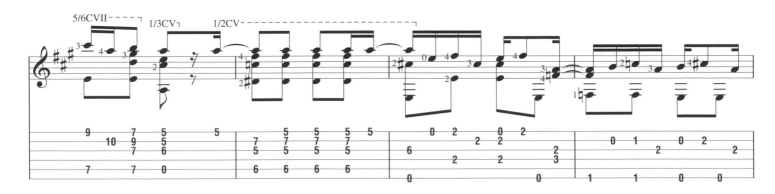

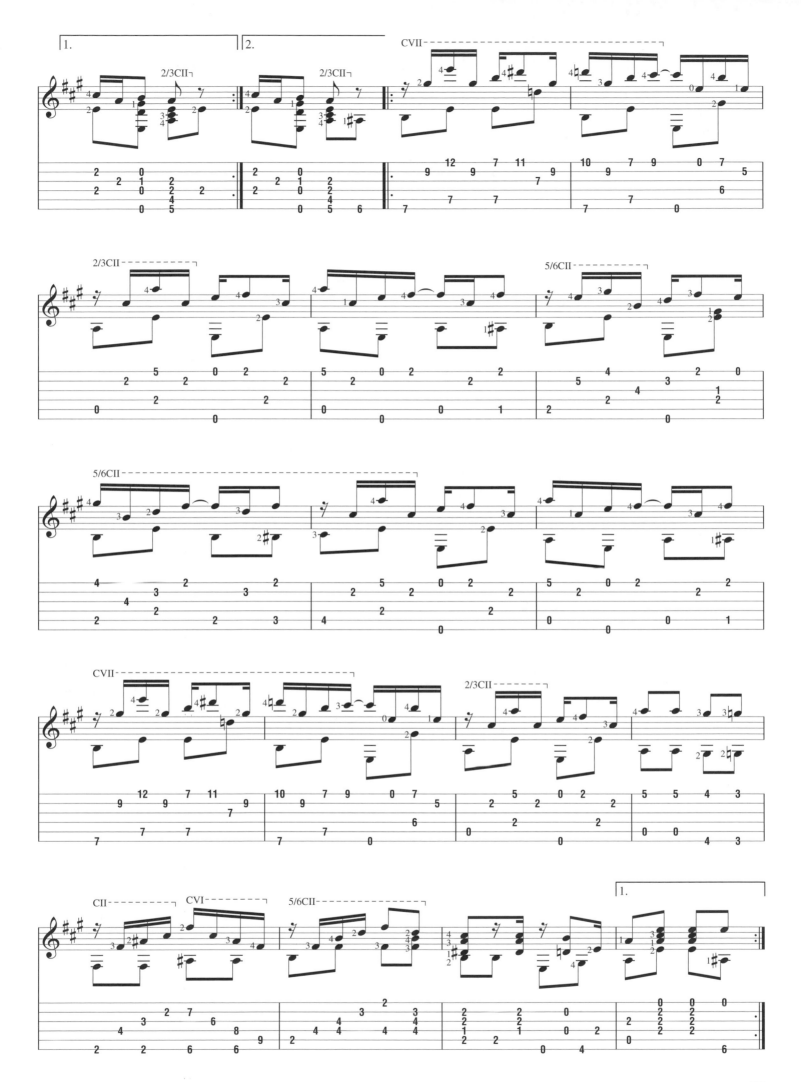

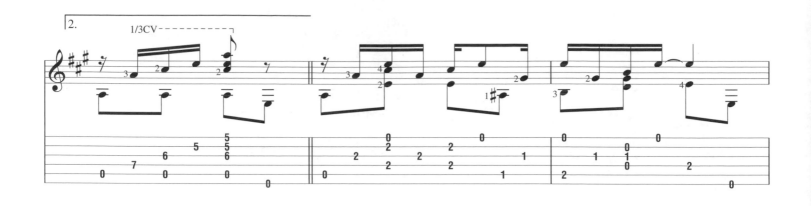

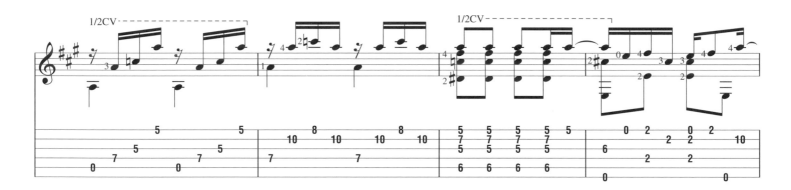

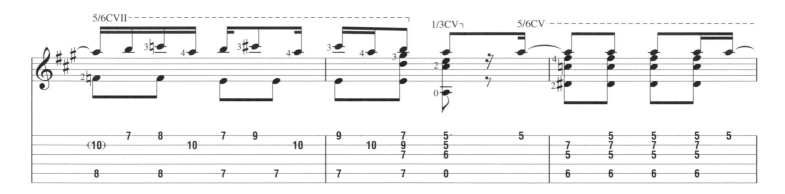

Moonlight Sonata

(Sonata Quasi Una Fantasia, Op. 27, No. 2 – First Movement)

By Ludwig van Beethoven
Transcribed for Guitar by Elias Barreiro

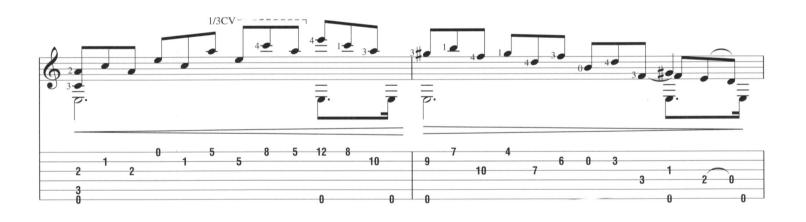

Minuet in G

By Johann Sebastian Bach
Arranged by Robert Henley Woody and Julius Bellson

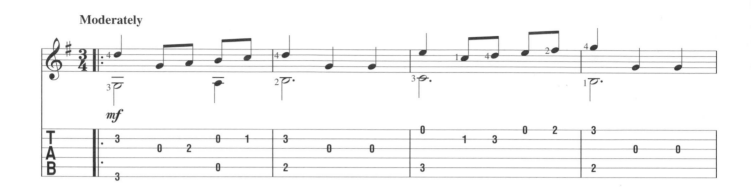

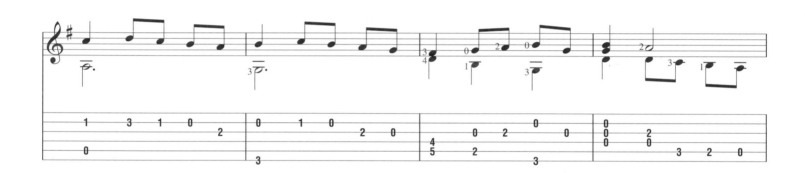

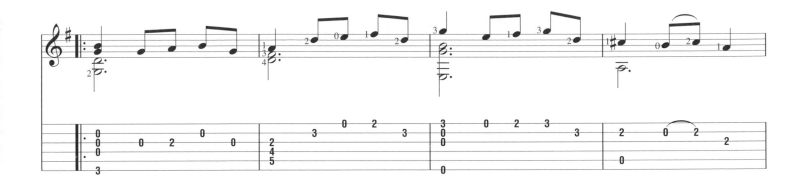

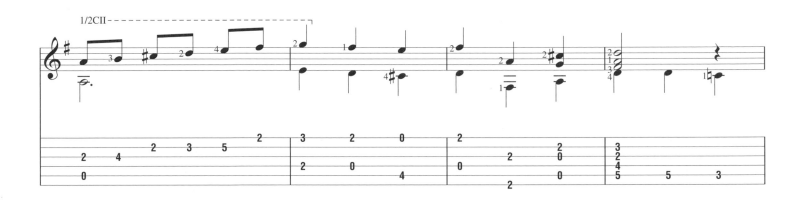

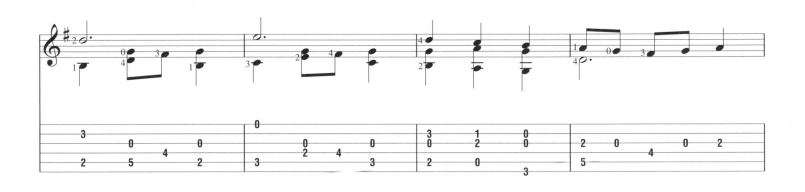

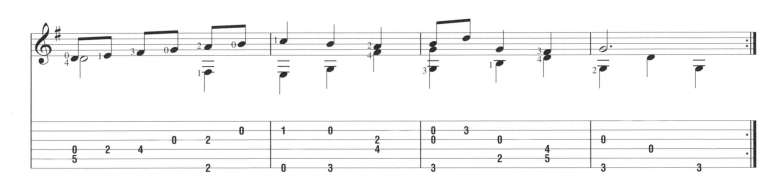

Prelude No. 1

from THE WELL-TEMPERED CLAVIER, BWV 846
By Johann Sebastian Bach
Transcribed for Guitar by Giovanni De Chiaro

Tuning:
(low to high) D-A-D-G-B-E

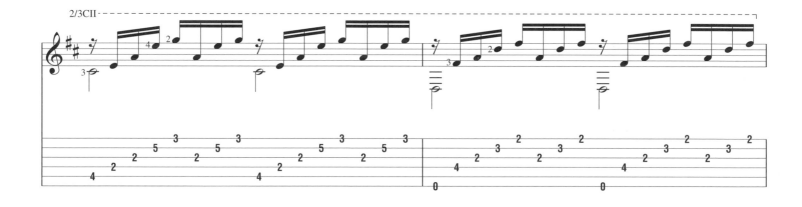

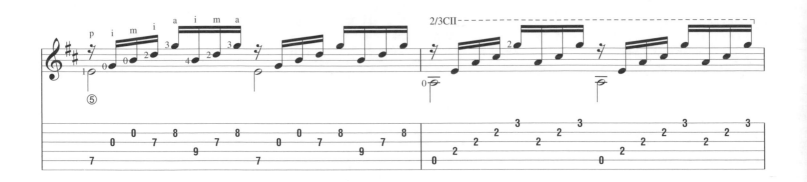

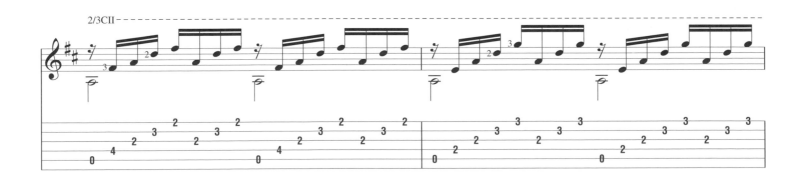

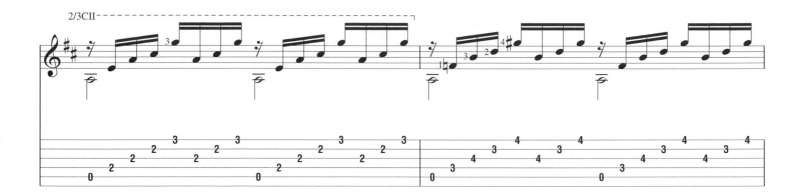

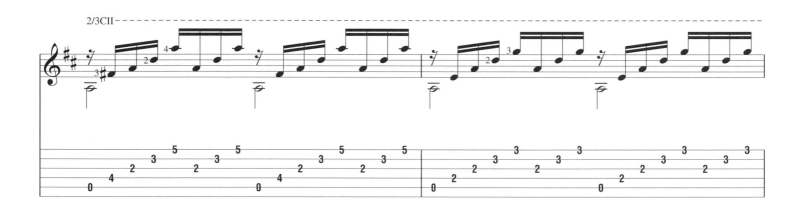

Rondeau

Theme from MASTERPIECE THEATER

By Jean Joseph Mouret

Transcribed for Guitar by Giovanni De Chiaro

Tuning:
(low to high) D-A-D-G-B-E

Moderately

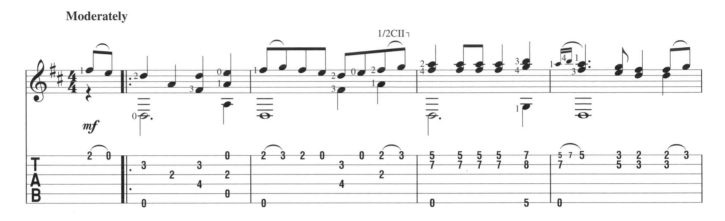

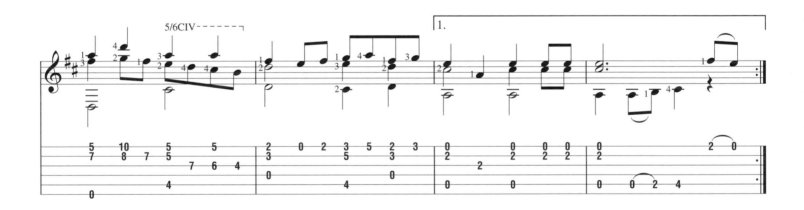

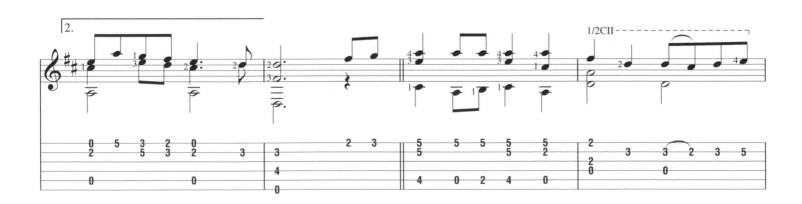

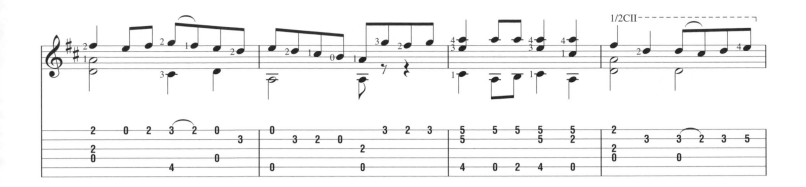

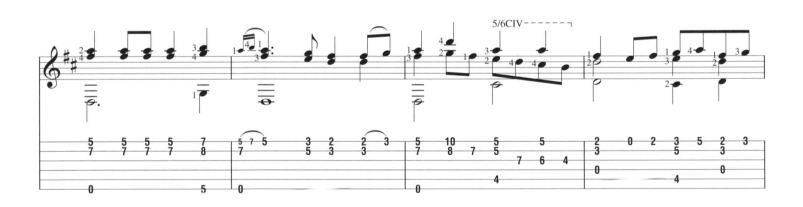

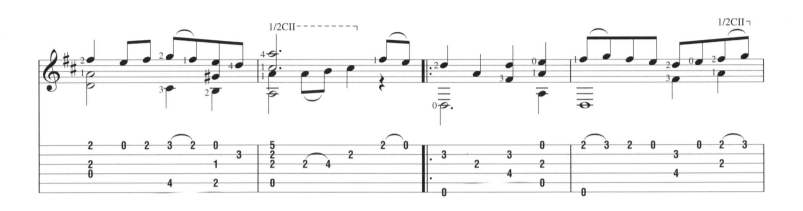

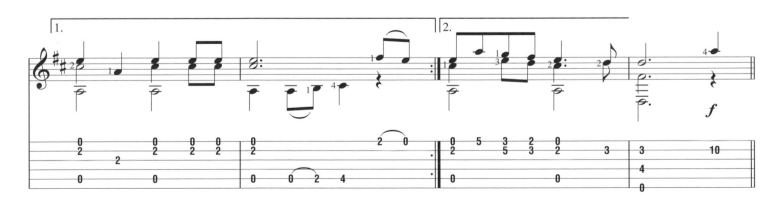

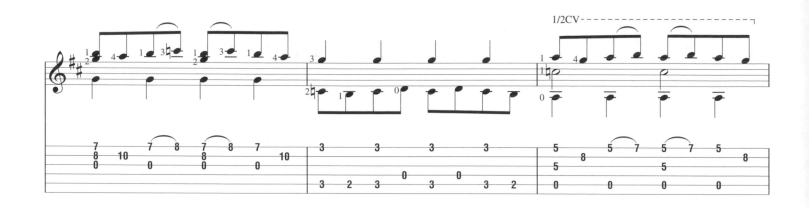

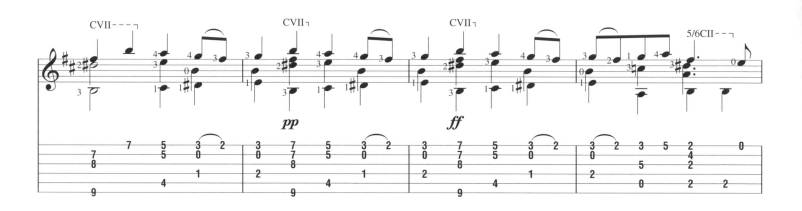

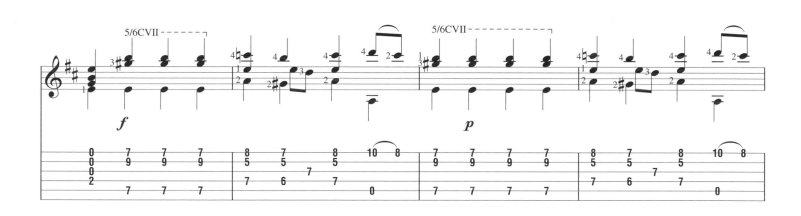

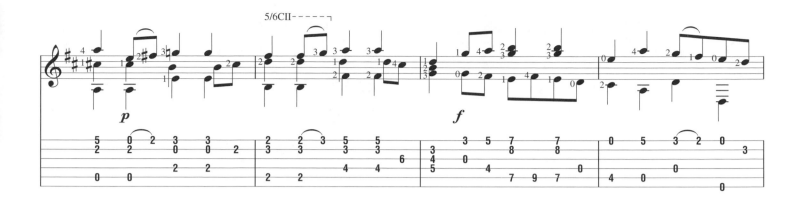

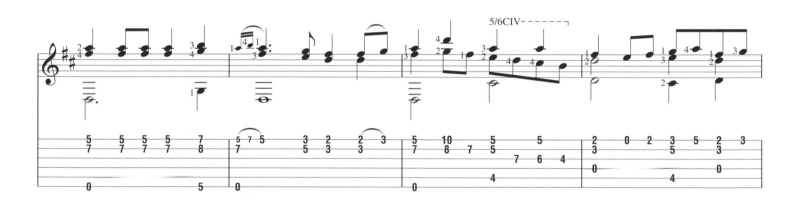

CLASSICAL GUITAR

THE BEATLES FOR CLASSICAL GUITAR

Includes 20 solos from big Beatles hits arranged for classical guitar, complete with left-hand and right-hand fingering. Songs include: All My Loving • And I Love Her • Can't Buy Me Love • Fool on the Hill • From a Window • Hey Jude • If I Fell • Let It Be • Michelle • Norwegian Wood • Obla Di • Ticket to Ride • Yesterday • and more. Features arrangements and an introduction by Joe Washington, as well as his helpful hints on classical technique and detailed notes on how to play each song. The book also covers parts and specifications of the classical guitar, tuning, and Joe's "Strata System" – an easy-reading system applied to chord diagrams.
00699237 Classical Guitar $19.99

CZERNY FOR GUITAR
12 SCALE STUDIES FOR CLASSICAL GUITAR
by David Patterson

INCLUDES TAB

Adapted from Carl Czerny's *School of Velocity, Op. 299* for piano, this lesson book explores 12 keys with 12 different approaches or "treatments." You will explore a variety of articulations, ranges and technical perspectives as you learn each key. These arrangements will not only improve your ability to play scales fluently, but will also develop your ears, knowledge of the fingerboard, reading abilities, strength and endurance. In standard notation and tablature.
00701248 ....$9.99

MATTEO CARCASSI – 25 MELODIC AND PROGRESSIVE STUDIES, OP. 60
arr. Paul Henry

One of Carcassi's (1792-1853) most famous collections of classical guitar music – indispensable for the modern guitarist's musical and technical development. Performed by Paul Henry. 49-minute audio accompaniment.
00696506 Book/Online Audio $17.99

CLASSICAL & FINGERSTYLE GUITAR TECHNIQUES

INCLUDES TAB

by David Oakes • Musicians Institute

This Master Class is aimed at any electric or acoustic guitarist who wants a quick, thorough grounding in the essentials of classical and fingerstyle technique. Topics covered include: arpeggios and scales, free stroke and rest stroke, P-i scale technique, three-to-a-string patterns, natural and artificial harmonics, tremolo and rasgueado, and more. The book includes 12 intensive lessons for right and left hand in standard notation & tab, and the audio features 92 solo acoustic tracks.
00695171 Book/Online Audio $17.99

CLASSICAL GUITAR CHRISTMAS COLLECTION

INCLUDES TAB

Includes classical guitar arrangements in standard notation and tablature for more than two dozen beloved carols: Angels We Have Heard on High • Auld Lang Syne • Ave Maria • Away in a Manger • Canon in D • The First Noel • God Rest Ye Merry, Gentlemen • Hark! the Herald Angels Sing • I Saw Three Ships • Jesu, Joy of Man's Desiring • Joy to the World • O Christmas Tree • O Holy Night • Silent Night • What Child Is This? • and more.
00699493 Guitar Solo $10.99

CLASSICAL GUITAR WEDDING

INCLUDES TAB

Perfect for players hired to perform for someone's big day, this songbook features 16 classsical wedding favorites arranged for solo guitar in standard notation and tablature. Includes: Air on the G String • Ave Maria • Bridal Chorus • Canon in D • Jesu, Joy of Man's Desiring • Minuet • Sheep May Safely Graze • Wedding March • and more.
00699563 Solo Guitar with Tab................................$12.99

CLASSICAL MASTERPIECES FOR GUITAR

INCLUDES TAB

27 works by Bach, Beethoven, Handel, Mendelssohn, Mozart and more transcribed with standard notation and tablature. Now anyone can enjoy classical material regardless of their guitar background. Also features stay-open binding.
00699312 ....$14.99

MASTERWORKS FOR GUITAR

INCLUDES TAB

Over 60 Favorites from Four Centuries
World's Great Classical Music

Dozens of classical masterpieces: Allemande • Bourree • Canon in D • Jesu, Joy of Man's Desiring • Lagrima • Malaguena • Mazurka • Piano Sonata No. 14 in C# Minor (Moonlight) Op. 27 No. 2 First Movement Theme • Ode to Joy • Prelude No. I (Well-Tempered Clavier).
00699503 ....$19.99

A MODERN APPROACH TO CLASSICAL GUITAR

by Charles Duncan

This multi-volume method was developed to allow students to study the art of classical guitar within a new, more contemporary framework. For private, class or self-instruction. Book One incorporates chord frames and symbols, as well as a recording to assist in tuning and to provide accompaniments for at-home practice. Book One also introduces beginning fingerboard technique and music theory. Book Two and Three build upon the techniques learned in Book One.
00695114 Book 1 – Book Only $6.99
00695113 Book 1 – Book/Online Audio................$10.99
00695116 Book 2 – Book Only $6.99
00695115 Book 2 – Book/Online Audio................$10.99
00699202 Book 3 – Book Only $9.99
00695117 Book 3 – Book/Online Audio................$12.99
00695119 Composite Book/CD Pack $29.99

ANDRES SEGOVIA – 20 STUDIES FOR GUITAR

Sor/Segovia

20 studies for the classical guitar written by Beethoven's contemporary, Fernando Sor, revised, edited and fingered by the great classical guitarist Andres Segovia. These essential repertoire pieces continue to be used by teachers and students to build solid classical technique. Features 50-minute demonstration audio.
00695012 Book/Online Audio $19.99
00006363 Book Only..$7.99

THE FRANCISCO COLLECTION TÁRREGA

INCLUDES TAB

edited and performed by Paul Henry

Considered the father of modern classical guitar, Francisco Tárrega revolutionized guitar technique and composed a wealth of music that will be a cornerstone of classical guitar repertoire for centuries to come. This unique book/audio pack features 14 of his most outstanding pieces in standard notation and tab, edited and performed by virtuoso Paul Henry. Includes: Adelita • Capricho Árabe • Estudio Brillante • Grand Jota • Lágrima • Malagueña • María • Recuerdos de la Alhambra • Tango • and more, plus bios of Tárrega and Henry.
00698993 Book/Online Audio $19.99

HAL•LEONARD®

Visit Hal Leonard Online at **www.halleonard.com**

Prices, contents and availability subject to change without notice.

FINGERPICKING GUITAR BOOKS

Hone your fingerpicking skills with these great songbooks featuring solo guitar arrangements in standard notation and tablature. The arrangements in these books are carefully written for intermediate-level guitarists. Each song combines melody and harmony in one superb guitar fingerpicking arrangement. Each book also includes an introduction to basic fingerstyle guitar.

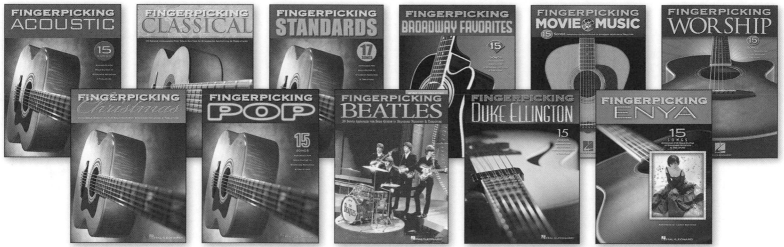

FINGERPICKING ACOUSTIC
00699614..............................$14.99

FINGERPICKING ACOUSTIC CLASSICS
00160211..............................$14.99

FINGERPICKING ACOUSTIC HITS
00160202..............................$12.99

FINGERPICKING ACOUSTIC ROCK
00699764..............................$12.99

FINGERPICKING BALLADS
00699717..............................$12.99

FINGERPICKING BEATLES
00699049..............................$19.99

FINGERPICKING BEETHOVEN
00702390................................$8.99

FINGERPICKING BLUES
00701277 ....$9.99

FINGERPICKING BROADWAY FAVORITES
00699843................................$9.99

FINGERPICKING BROADWAY HITS
00699838................................$7.99

FINGERPICKING CELTIC FOLK
00701148..............................$10.99

FINGERPICKING CHILDREN'S SONGS
00699712................................$9.99

FINGERPICKING CHRISTIAN
00701076 ....$7.99

FINGERPICKING CHRISTMAS
00699599................................$9.99

FINGERPICKING CHRISTMAS CLASSICS
00701695................................$7.99

FINGERPICKING CHRISTMAS SONGS
00171333..............................$9.99

FINGERPICKING CLASSICAL
00699620..............................$10.99

FINGERPICKING COUNTRY
00699687..............................$10.99

FINGERPICKING DISNEY
00699711..............................$15.99

FINGERPICKING EARLY JAZZ STANDARDS
00276565 ....$12.99

FINGERPICKING DUKE ELLINGTON
00699845................................$9.99

FINGERPICKING ENYA
00701161..............................$10.99

FINGERPICKING FILM SCORE MUSIC
00160143..............................$12.99

FINGERPICKING GOSPEL
00701059................................$9.99

FINGERPICKING GUITAR BIBLE
00691040 ....$19.99

FINGERPICKING HIT SONGS
00160195..............................$12.99

FINGERPICKING HYMNS
00699688................................$9.99

FINGERPICKING IRISH SONGS
00701965................................$9.99

FINGERPICKING ITALIAN SONGS
00159778..............................$12.99

FINGERPICKING JAZZ FAVORITES
00699844................................$9.99

FINGERPICKING JAZZ STANDARDS
00699840..............................$10.99

FINGERPICKING ELTON JOHN
00237495..............................$12.99

FINGERPICKING LATIN FAVORITES
00699842................................$9.99

FINGERPICKING LATIN STANDARDS
00699837..............................$12.99

FINGERPICKING ANDREW LLOYD WEBBER
00699839..............................$14.99

FINGERPICKING LOVE SONGS
00699841..............................$12.99

FINGERPICKING LOVE STANDARDS
00699836 ....$9.99

FINGERPICKING LULLABYES
00701276................................$9.99

FINGERPICKING MOVIE MUSIC
00699919..............................$10.99

FINGERPICKING MOZART
00699794................................$9.99

FINGERPICKING POP
00699615..............................$12.99

FINGERPICKING POPULAR HITS
00139079..............................$12.99

FINGERPICKING PRAISE
00699714..............................$10.99

FINGERPICKING ROCK
00699716..............................$12.99

FINGERPICKING STANDARDS
00699613..............................$12.99

FINGERPICKING WEDDING
00699637................................$9.99

FINGERPICKING WORSHIP
00700554..............................$10.99

FINGERPICKING NEIL YOUNG – GREATEST HITS
00700134..............................$14.99

FINGERPICKING YULETIDE
00699654................................$9.99

HAL•LEONARD®

Visit Hal Leonard online at **www.halleonard.com**

Prices, contents and availability
subject to change without notice.